TENNIS
Playing, Training and Winning

TENNIS
Playing, Training and Winning

Marcel Gautschi

ARCO PUBLISHING COMPANY, INC.
New York

Published 1979 by Arco Publishing Company, Inc.
219 Park Avenue South, New York, N.Y. 10003

Printed in Great Britain

Library of Congress Cataloging in Publication Data
Gautschi, Marcel.
    Tennis, playing, training, and winning.

    1. Tennis.   I. Title.
GV995.G34   796.34'22   78-17159
ISBN 0-668-04692-9
ISBN 0-668-04700-3 pbk

Contents

Author's Foreword   6

Playing
Concentrating and Relaxing   9
Running and Positioning   11
Serving   13
Service return   20
Passing shot   27
Playing from the baseline   28
Forehand and backhand   34
Lob   40
Drop shot   44
Attacking, advancing, playing at the net   48
Volley   56
Half volley   58
Smash   59
Doubles   62

Training
Assessing your weaknesses   73
Personal assessment   76
Working on your weaknesses   83
Competition training   91
Mental training and learning by spectating   93
Fitness   95

Winning
The little things that count   103
Overcome nervousness, adopt a positive attitude   107
Knowing yourself and your opponent   112
Nine different players and how to play against them   115
Awkward situations   130
Wind, sun, bad court conditions   135
Lost – what now?   138
Assessment by a third party   142

Glossary of technical terms   143
Bibliography   144

2032240

Author's Foreword

If your aims are to play tennis more skilfully and to win more often, then this is the right book for you. Each sentence has one aim in view: *to help you get the most out of your tennis.*

Good technique alone is not a sure passport to victory, and a complete change of style is very rarely necessary. In the section 'Playing', you will therefore find, not a detailed discussion of technique, but a number of simple points to help you improve your strokes and tactics.

If you want to improve your game, your training must be geared to your weaknesses. (This is true of almost all sports.)

With the help of this book, you can follow a sensible training programme, by investigating your game point by point with the personal assessment chart (see pages 76–82) and by concentrating your training on the faults pinpointed, with the help of the exercises given.

This book has been written for the competitive player whose aim is primarily to win. Knowing how to:

prepare for a match;
conquer your nerves;
take advantage of your opponent's weaknesses;
beat difficult opponents;
play your best tennis at crucial moments;
defy wind and sun; and
get over a defeat,

are just as important for tennis as good services or backhand volleys.

If tennis is more to you than just a pastime, you will work with this book, you will consult it during training and before any important match. (Left-handers must make allowances for the fact that the book is aimed at their rather more common opposite numbers; similarly, for the sake of simplicity, I have described the player as 'he' rather than as 'he or she'.)

Playing

Concentrating and Relaxing

1 Concentrating on the
ball.

Concentration is the ability to
ignore any outside factors which
might hinder the execution of a
certain action, and to devote one-
self fully to one's task.

When it is applied to tennis,
concentration means following the
ball – *from the moment it has left
your opponent's racket right up to
the moment when you hit it* – and
ignoring any factors which may be
physically or mentally disturbing,
such as the opponent, spectators,
previous poor shots, the weather.

One rarely finds a tennis coach who
does not feel that the ability to
concentrate in this way is essential.
Keeping one's eye on the ball is
recognised also by top-class
players as a decisive factor. It is a
part of self-discipline, which even
the greatest talent cannot ignore.
Your ability to concentrate on the
ball is revealed in particularly tricky
situations, e.g., after a bad decision.
If, at such a moment, you allow
your thoughts to stray from the
matter in hand you will surely lose.
If you succeed in ignoring all
disturbing outside factors, not even
a bad decision will put you off your
rhythm.

A similar problem arises when
playing crucial points. At such
moments, many players concentrate
their thoughts on the two
alternatives of victory and defeat,
with the result that they become
very tense. If they simply
concentrated on the ball they would
stay relaxed and be better able to
control the situation.

Concentrating and Relaxing

Billie Jean King's
concentration exercise.

If you have trouble in following the
ball, the exercise which gave Billie
Jean King her fabulous ability to
concentrate may be of help to you:
Before an important game she
would fix her eyes on a tennis ball
for about ten minutes without
interruption and without thinking of
anything else.

2 Concentrating on your
opponent and the game.

Observation and analysis of your
opponent and the game go hand in
hand with observation of the ball.
Most players regard the ability to
anticipate the direction and depth
of the opponent's strokes as a gift
rather than as a skill.

Anticipation usually only involves
knowing your opponent's stroke
repertoire and characteristic moves,
and using this knowledge to predict
his return of your own shots:

Has he mastered the backhand
played down the line?
Does he use the lob at all?
Does he advance on short balls or
does he remain at the back of the
court?

Knowing the answers to such
questions enables you to recognise,
right from the start, what you must
expect in a given situation. In
addition, the position of his feet,
his racket or his left arm can give
clues to his intentions.
It goes without saying that you must
not watch your opponent for too
long. As soon as it has left his
racket devote all your attention to
the ball.

Running and Positioning

Running hard is not enough.

Despite their superb running ability, many players regularly reach the ball too late.

Being on the alert involves:

rapidly recognising the opponent's stroke;

reacting and running quickly; and immediately returning to the correct court position after the stroke.

React in plenty of time.

You must act as soon as the ball leaves your opponent's racket. By the time you act you should already have recognised the direction and depth of your opponent's stroke. Close concentration on the ball and a knowledge of his game favour fast reaction.

Standing to receive the ball.

To be able to run to the left or to the right:

the weight of your body must be on the balls of your feet;

your heels must not touch the ground;

your body must be ready to spring into action; and

your knees must be bent.

Running and Positioning

Retreating when the opponent plays a deep return.

Many players can run well forwards or sideways. However, if a long ball comes straight at them, they stand rooted to the spot instead of *retreating immediately* and then advancing to the ball.

After the shot, go straight back to the centre of the possible returns.

Do not just stand still after the stroke: *run* back to the centre of the possible returns.

The centre is the point from which you are best ready to return any of your opponent's possible shots.

Just where the centre actually lies differs from case to case (see Service return; Playing from the baseline; Attacking, advancing, playing at the net).

Serving

Practise your service as often as possible.

The service is the most important stroke in tennis.

The server has an enormous advantage because he is the first to determine the direction, speed and spin of the ball. If he can make skilful and surprising use of this advantage, his opponent will be forced to play a defensive game right from the start.

It is therefore worth paying special attention to your service and practising it as often as possible— if necessary without a partner— since it gets too little attention during normal training.

Serving

Seventy per cent of your first service should go into the service box.

Do you smash your first service?

If the answer is yes, remember that seventy per cent of your first services should land in the service box. If your quota is below that, you would do well to sacrifice some of your speed for the sake of consistency. Nothing shows how weak a player is more than a rare cannonball as the first service and a soft ball as the second service.

Avoid a second service in crucial situations.

When playing for game, set or match, your first service should be a good one to avoid the need for a second service and spare your nerves for a possibly tricky volley.

Play to your opponent's backhand, but not all the time.

Most players have difficulties with their backhand return, and a forehand return can be more viciously angled.

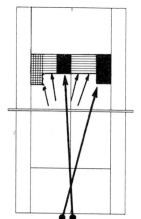

Two thirds of your services should therefore be aimed at the opponent's backhand. The remaining third is aimed either:

at his forehand (especially effective if you are serving from the right-hand side of the court); or straight at him.

This way he will never have the opportunity to prepare himself for the backhand.

On crucial points, tacticians always play to their opponent's backhand.

Serving

Vary spin and speed
whenever possible.

Your service will be most effective
if you vary not only the direction
but also the spin and speed of the
ball.

After a series of hard services,
you should occasionally slip in a
strongly angled slice, providing of
course that you possess the
necessary technical ability. Varying
your service will make your
opponent uncertain whether to
position himself further back,
further forward, further to the right
or to the left for the return.

Depth of your second
service.

Your opponent has a significant
psychological advantage on your
second service: he knows that your
ball must land in the service box so
he is much more relaxed.

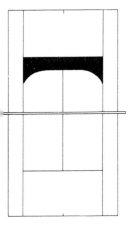

The most important rule here is to
remember *depth.* Nothing will
encourage your opponent more
than being given the chance to
leave you stranded after a short
second service. Your only answer
to this lies in a high quota of
successful first services and second
services played deep (best of all
hit with a little slice or spin).

Serving

Relax!

Tension can be particularly dangerous on the service, when the ball must land in one quarter of the court. To avoid becoming tense, remember the following tips:

hold the racket loosely in your hand;

breathe out deeply before every service; and

take your time. (This is especially important for the second service.)

Begin slowly.

Your muscles must be completely relaxed before you can serve aces.

Therefore you should loosen up your arm muscles before a game, begin slowly, and *gradually* build up the speed of your service.

Correct stance.

To be able to place the service, you must position yourself so that your left shoulder and your racket are pointing in the direction you wish to serve the ball.

Serving

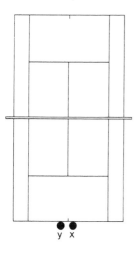

y x

The (back) right foot should be parallel to the baseline, the (front) left foot should point slightly towards the net.

The best places to position yourself are: on the forehand side, as close as possible to the centre of the court (x); and, on the backhand side, about a yard (one metre) left of the centre (y).

From these positions you can aim with precision at your opponent's backhand and you will need to move only a short distance sideways to be ready for every possible return.

Correct toss.

During the service the left arm plays an important rôle. The whole rhythm of the service is grievously affected by a ball which is tossed too far to the right or left, or forwards or backwards. The path followed by the left arm forms the basis of the service and should be practised separately if this is your weak point.

NB   Tossing the ball involves, not a circular, but rather a straight movement upwards of the left arm. The ball must be released from the fingertips when the arm is completely straight, so that the ball travels the minimum possible distance, with the maximum amount of accuracy.

17

Serving

Throw the racket head up to the ball.

When the ball has almost reached its highest point, the racket is raised energetically from its position behind your head, and brought forward to hit the ball.

Hit the ball when it is at its highest position.

To achieve maximum effect, contact between racket and ball must occur *at the highest possible point*, the right arm and the racket forming a straight line.

Snap with your wrist.

After the moment of contact, the wrist is snapped forward (as when throwing a ball).

It is this pronounced snap action, rather than sheer muscle power, which gives speed to the service.

Serving

Weight transference.

The weight which is on the right foot at the start of the service is transferred on to the left foot during the toss.

To give the ball additional travel, step forward onto your right foot after the ball has been struck.

The correct weight transfer is: right to left to right.

Service Return

Factors which influence the return.

The reason for the service return being such a difficult stroke is that it varies according to the

speed;
spin; and
direction
of the service.

A question to consider before returning your opponent's service is:

has he stayed at the back of the court after his service or has he advanced to the net?

The following points are valid for all service returns.

Besides having a versatile return, there are other points which need to be taken into account.

1 The ready position.

The position you stand in to receive the service should enable you to run left or right in a fraction of a second.

You should have:

the upper part of your body leaning slightly forwards;

your knees flexed;

your feet parallel, between twelve and eighteen inches (thirty to forty-five centimetres apart);

your left hand on the neck of the racket, and your racket pointing slightly to the left;

your weight on the balls of your feet; and

your whole body relaxed, swaying slightly.

Service Return

2 Concentrate on the ball.

Your aim should be to recognise the direction of the service at the very latest when the ball has just left your opponent's racket.
So concentrate only on the ball *from the moment your opponent tosses it to serve.*

3 Begin your backswing as early as possible.

Begin your backswing as soon as you have recognised whether the ball is going towards your forehand or your backhand.

4 Short backswing.

The quicker the service, the shorter the backswing.

5 Shoulder pointing at the net.

Should you have insufficient time to make your shot with the correct foot forward, you must at least turn the upper part of your body so that either your left (for the forehand) or right shoulder (for the backhand) is pointing towards the net. This is the only way you can hit the ball in the required direction.

Service Return

6 'Attack' the ball and hit it when it is still in front of your body.

Immediately before the moment of contact, your body weight is transferred forward to receive the ball. Do not allow yourself to be forced backwards even by the hardest of services.

7 Watch your opponent when he tosses the ball.

Very few players can hit flat, kick or slice services without letting their opponent know their intention in advance. *The toss* (normal=flat service, to the left=kick, to the right=slice) *will usually betray the spin and therefore also the direction of the ball.*

The position of the body and racket, as well as the individual habits of the server (the way he gets ready, how he begins his backswing, etc.) give the returner valuable indications as to the direction and type of service being attempted.

Service return, forehand

Service Return

Service return, backhand

Returning a hard service.

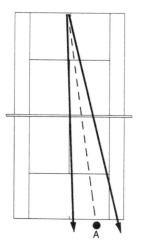

Only top-class players can receive a very hard service at baseline level without being overwhelmed by the force of the ball.

If your reflexes are not of the fastest, you may safely position yourself about one yard (one metre) behind the baseline, at point A on the diagram (so that you have an equal distance left or right to run). This way you can use your weight to give power to your return.

If you try to return hard services with even harder shots, your quota of errors will be high. Frequently, simply blocking the ball ('chipping' it) is the best solution. For this stroke, the racket is brought into the path of the ball with the wrist kept stiff (as in the volley).

23

Service Return

Returning a kick service.

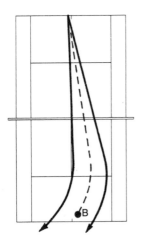

The kick service bounces high and is most effective when it is aimed at the backhand. You will almost always recognise it in advance, because your opponent tosses the ball up to his left (your right).

Position yourself as far forward as possible (point B on the diagram) to receive the ball as it rises and simultaneously 'attack' it.

If you stay back and allow the ball to come to you, its spin will over-whelm you.

Returning a slice service.

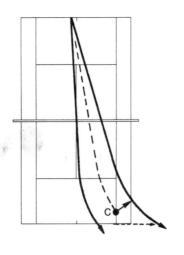

The slice service bounces low, and is aimed at the forehand. It is played usually onto the right-hand side of the court to force the receiver off the court.

If your opponent tosses the ball to his right (your left) you can position yourself in plenty of time. Stand level with point C on the diagram. The nearer you stand to the back of the court, the further the distance to the ball.

Finally:
So as not to be forced right off the court, reduce the angle of such a service by running forwards diagonally instead of parallel to the baseline.

Service Return

If your opponent stays on the baseline after serving.

If your opponent stays on the baseline after a hard service, your best stroke is a return hit high and as deep as possible into the centre of the court, because it gives you enough time to regain the centre of the court.

Your best answer to a soft, short service is a deep, attacking shot played down the line.

No mistakes are allowed on such a simple shot. Remember that you are playing close to the net and the ball could well go out if you hit it as hard as if you were still on the baseline.

On the right-hand side of the court you can, of course, run round the ball, to put pressure on your opponent with your forehand. (On the left-hand side you would be forced off the court.)

If your opponent advances after serving.

A good return is a consistent return. The desire always to place the ball past an opponent advancing to the net leads to countless errors. However, if you manage to keep the ball in play you have almost a fifty-fifty chance of winning the point. Stick to the basic rules listed overleaf.

Service Return

1 Concentrate on the ball, not on your opponent.

Pay absolutely no attention to your opponent if he advances to the net, or he will inevitably influence your shots. Devote all your attention to the ball.

2 Try to keep the return low.

Your return should bounce somewhere along the service line. A short stroke has already passed the peak of its trajectory when it crosses the net (see diagram).

3 Vary your returns.

Your opponent should not be able to accustom himself to a certain rhythm:

Direct your shots not only to his left or right but also *straight at him.* No player likes a ball aimed at his feet. Moreover, with this return there is no risk of the ball going out of court at the sides.

The high lob is a good change-of-pace shot. If you are hard-pressed, it is your only way out. With this shot you definitely have a better chance of regaining control of the volley and winning the point than you have with a daring passing shot.

assing Shot

he three basic rules.

Never try a passing shot when hard-pressed.

The effect on you will be the same whether your opponent advances to the net after an attacking shot or after serving. Therefore the three basic rules, which hold good for the service return (opposite) are also true in the case of the passing shot:

1 Keep your eye on the ball, never on your opponent.

2 Try to keep the ball low.

3 Play straight at him occasionally, instead of only to his right or left.

If you can only reach the ball with difficulty, there is only one answer: a high lob.

You won't get as much applause, but you will have infinitely more chance of winning points with a high lob than you would with a passing shot.

Playing from the Baseline

Consistency.

Clever tacticians know that in base line play they can win no straight points when playing against an opponent who is a powerful runner Therefore they take no unnecessary risks and endeavour primarily to *keep the ball in play.*

Depth.

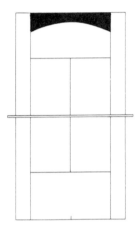

A short ball is received almost as gratefully by your opponent as a mishit because:

you give him the opportunity and plenty of time to build up an attack and chase you pitilessly around the court;

you have too little time to get ready for the next ball; and

you have to run further to reach the ball because your opponent can force you off the court with an angled shot.

This is why *depth is a decisive factor in baseline play.* With deep balls *you* put your opponent under pressure by forcing him to return just as deep.

Play the ball high enough over the net.

Do your baseline shots have a flat trajectory? If so, then your shots will frequently end up in the net or be too short.

Your game will gain consistency and depth if you place your shots over the net with an adequate safety margin (at least a yard—that is nearly a metre).

28

Playing from the Baseline

The rule in baseline play is to concentrate on not allowing the ball to end up in the net. You will be astonished how much trouble your opponent will have with relatively high balls.

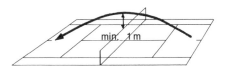

After each shot get back to the centre of any possible returns.

Immediately after each shot you must find the point on the court from which you have the same distance to run (left or right) according to the two possible returns by your opponent.

On the diagram, this point lies along line W which bisects the angle (a) between the two service side lines a and a_1.

The centre of the possible returns is the centre of the court only if your opponent plays from the centre. In all other cases it is in the right- or left-hand side of the court.

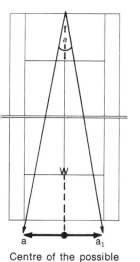

Centre of the possible returns.

Playing from the Baseline

After a shot played down the line you must run parallel to the baseline *beyond* the centre mark.

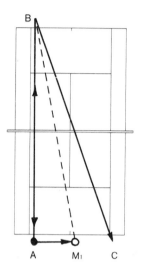

Let us suppose that you have played a ball from point A to point B on to your opponent's forehand.

Your opponent now has the choice of either playing back to point A or aiming for point C. The centre of these two possible returns is at point M_1, just on your forehand.

After a crosscourt shot, stop *before* the centre mark.

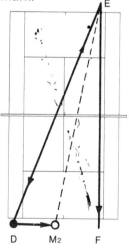

You now play from D to E on to your opponent's backhand. Your opponent can either play back to D or to F. The centre of possible returns now lies on your backhand at point M_2.

If you had played a down-the-line shot from point D, you would have had to cross the centre mark; i.e., run at least two extra steps.

Thus, in order to be in the strongest possible position for your opponent's return, the distance you have to run is shorter after a crosscourt shot than it is after a down-the-line shot.

Playing from the Baseline

he centre depends also the centre depends also n your opponent.

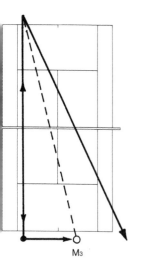

M₃

When playing against opponents who can play a forehand cross-court shot (which forces you off the court), angle (a) becomes greater and the centre (M_3) moves even further on to your forehand side.

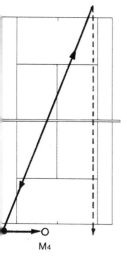

M₄

On the other hand, you only need to move to point M_4 after your cross-court shot, if you have spotted that your opponent has not yet mastered the backhand played down the line.

A knowledge of your opponent's strengths and weaknesses will therefore influence your choice of position.

Playing from the Baseline

The crosscourt shot is easier and safer than the shot played down the line.

If you play the ball across the court you have two advantages: you can hit the ball further—because of the extra length of the diagonal—and lower—because the height of the net is least in the middle. The crosscourt shot is therefore considered the classic baseline shot.

Even if positioning and execution of the shot are imperfect, the crosscourt ball is more likely to land in the court than the down-the-line one, which is why it is the best shot to play:

if you have no time to get into the best position to receive the ball; or if you have trouble in finding your rhythm.
(The longer flight path also allows you to prepare yourself better for the next shot.)

Occasionally play a ball short across court.

If you occasionally play a short diagonal shot after a number of long shots, you will force your opponent off court and have an empty field of play for your next shot.

It goes without saying that this tactic presupposes complete mastery of the technique.

Playing from the Baseline

When under pressure play high.

If your opponent puts pressure on you with fast, well placed shots, it is pointless trying to adapt yourself to his rhythm: you will only end up making too many mistakes.

In such a situation, high balls played deep into the centre at the back of his court have the following advantages:

they give you enough time to reach the centre of the possible returns;

your opponent can only angle such shots with difficulty; and

he is thrown off rhythm.

Forehand and Backhand

The different styles all
have points in common.

There is no such thing as *the*
correct fore- or back-hand stroke.

One top-class player may use the
Eastern, the other the Continental
grip, one may swing back in a
circular motion, the other in a
straight line, one may hit with top
spin, another with slice; and you
can reach the top by playing with
one or both hands.

Nevertheless all the techniques
have rules in common.

Swing back early.

Remember to bring your racket
back as early as possible.

The backswing begins when the
ball has just left your opponent's
racket and you have recognised its
direction.

Even on slow shots you must not
start any later. The rhythm of the
backswing is suited to the speed of
the ball, so that there is no pause or
hesitation in the movement.

Forehand and Backhand

Backswing on the run.

Swinging back early is especially vital with shots you have to run for.

Begin your backswing with the *first* step of your run, so that you only need to swing your racket forwards when you reach the ball.

2032240

Short backswing.

If you wish to return fast balls, your backswing must be *as short as possible.*

The basic rule is: Do not swing the racket back any more than is necessary for your body, right arm and racket to form a straight line at right angles to the net.

Long backswings are inadvisable for the following reasons:

they are less safe because of the greater distance travelled by the racket to reach the ball;

contact with the ball is made late because of the long time taken to complete the action; and
the immense sweep throws the body off-balance.

If you put your weight into the ball, your shots will develop enough power even with short backswings.

Forehand and Backhand

As little wrist action as
possible.

If you value safe strokes more than
occasional 'winners', you should
use as little wrist action as possible
when hitting the ball.

Only very talented players can
afford to snap their wrists without
losing control of the ball when
doing so, since such subtle
variations in movement decide the
success or failure of such a shot.

The line of your shoulders
should be at right angles
to the net.

Your shoulders should form a
straight line with the spot towards
which you are aiming the ball.

If you pull your racket back with
both hands at the start of your
backswing, the line of your
shoulders will automatically
become perpendicular to the net.

Attack the ball.

There is a world of difference
between waiting for the ball to
reach you and advancing to meet it.
*There is no surer way of losing the
initiative and thus the game, than
simply waiting for the ball to come
to you.*

If your opponent bombards you
with deep shots, position yourself
one or two yards (one or two
metres) behind the baseline, but
always run *towards the ball.*

Forehand and Backhand

Put the weight of your body into the ball.

Immediately before the stroke, the weight of the body is transferred on to the front foot — left for the forehand and right for the backhand. The body should lean towards the spot at which you are aiming the ball.

Only in emergencies should you transfer your weight sideways or play shots off the wrong foot. Since the weight of the body has not been put behind the ball, such shots have no force.

Point of contact in front of you.

Most players' shots lose a little control and speed because the ball is struck too late.

Only if the point of contact between ball and racket is in front of the body can you

observe the ball at the moment of contact without having to turn your head backwards and put your weight behind the ball.

Hitting the ball when it is in front of you does not mean taking it as it rises. This requires a lot of talent and training and is only recommended in exceptional circumstances (returning a service which bounces high or unexpectedly fast ball).

Forehand and Backhand

Follow the stroke through.

The longer you follow the stroke through and 'keep' the ball on the racket, the more control you will have over the shot.

In the follow-through swing your arm forwards loosely until it is fully outstretched.

Stay where you are.

When following the stroke through, remain in the position which you assumed to begin with. The back foot must on no account be brought forward. The stroke must be played from a stable position.

Players who jerk their bodies round after making contact lose all control over the shot and unintentionally send the ball across court or out at the sides.

You can tell whether your follow-through is long enough and made from a stable position by holding your position immediately after the stroke.

Forehand and Backhand

Forehand

Backhand

Lob

A much despised shot.

In the eyes of many tennis players lobs are boring even unfair shots only to be played in exceptional circumstances.

But most top-class players would not agree; after all, your opponent can also take advantage of this useful weapon, and he can return your lob with a spectacular smash. Successful tacticians have recognised the many applications of the lob and play it much more frequently than the average player.

When playing against overwhelmingly powerful attackers the lob is often the only effective weapon. You should therefore consider whether you want to go out in a blaze of glory with risky passing shots or to make a real contest out of the match by challenging your opponent with systematic lobs.

The following are examples of some of the situations in which the lob really does have to recommend itself:

The shot when you are hard-pressed.

If you can just reach a ball but cannot get it fully under control, then you *must* lob, since only a high ball will give you time to return to the centre of possible returns.

In this situation your lob should be hit very high. Even if such a ball bounces in the centre of the court, your opponent needs strong nerves and a lot of concentration to win a point off it.

Lob

Statistics show that your chances of winning a point, when you have been forced to the edge of the court, are approximately three times better with a lob than with a normal stroke played in desperation.

The lob as a rhythm breaker.

Is your opponent constantly on the attack?
Does he come very close to the net, enabling him to attack passing shots by volleying downwards?

If so, then you *must* throw in the occasional lob or his attacking shots will overwhelm you.

Even if your opponent does not advance to the net, high balls will prevent him from settling into the rhythm of his game.

The lob as a substitute for a passing shot.

Do you have only a weak backhand passing shot or, worse, no real backhand at all?

If so, there is no sense in handing your opponent the points on a plate right from the very start.

Do you simply not feel on form?

In that case most of your passing shots will fail because you will feel harassed by your opponent and your shots will be uncontrolled.

In both cases the lob is the only sensible solution.

Have you got sufficient self-confidence to use it judiciously?

Lob

Follow your lob to the net.

By no means a ridiculous idea.

Your opponent will betray a lot of discomfort, especially on his backhand, when faced with an attacking ball.

If he is not a really experienced player, the only sensible reply left to him is a counter-lob.

You should be ready for this right from the start.

Lobbing into the sun.

A dirty trick?

Your reluctance to lob into the sun will vanish when it brings you points — after all, you are playing to win!

Play high lobs deep enough.

After it has reached its highest point, the high lob drops almost vertically to the ground. You must take this fact into account and aim to have the ball reach its highest point above the service line and not above the net.

As a result your high lobs will have enough depth.

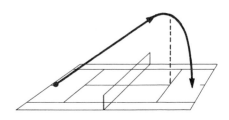

.ob

Aim at your opponent's backhand.

Your opponent will have trouble with this shot both at the net and at the back of the court.

.ong, upward follow-hrough.

Ending the stroke prematurely is the most common cause of unsuccessful lobs.

The longer you follow the stroke through and keep the ball on your racket the better.

Only for the real experts: he attacking lob.

In the attacking lob, the ball is played at a relatively high speed to pass only slightly above the opponent's racket.

Such a stroke requires the use of the wrist, which is flicked downwards after the racket touches the ball. In this way the ball looks as though it is going out but the spin makes it drop to the ground just short of the baseline.

Top-class players use the attacking lob only when they feel in peak form.

Drop Shot

Drop shots are not absolutely necessary.

The drop shot is not an essential. It requires a *very sensitive touch*, since little is needed to make the shot a success or a failure. A drop shot which is hit too deep, which bounces too high or which is telegraphed is fatal.

The racket face is placed under the ball.

The first stage in the drop shot is the slice. Immediately after the moment of contact, the wrist begins to turn, so that the racket face comes to rest directly below the ball; as a result the ball bounces back awkwardly as it lands. At the end of the stroke the racket face points upwards. The shot is followed through with a very delicate touch, but the racket must not swing out as it would with a ground stroke.

Hit the ball when it is still well in front of you.

Contact with the ball must be made as far as possible in front of the body. Only in this way will your stroke have the necessary delicacy of touch.

Pretend to hit a ground stroke.

If your opponent recognises your intention as a result of your back-swing, the effect of the drop shot will be lost.

You will preserve the essential element of surprise by pretending you are planning a ground stroke.

Drop Shot

Don't consider the point won too soon.

Don't lull yourself into a false feeling of security after a successful drop shot, but run straight back to the centre of possible returns. Your opponent may have correctly predicted your intention.

The drop shot as an attacking shot.

It is possible to disguise a drop shot as a long attacking ball to be followed to the net.

Your opponent will have difficulty in getting the ball past you if you are positioned far enough forward.

Five situations unsuited to the drop shot:

1 Deep shots

A drop shot played from the baseline is too risky. Moreover the ball would be in the air for so long that your opponent would be able to reach it with little trouble.

2 Hard Shots

The drop shot must be 'held' on the racket for as long as possible, and this cannot be done when answering hard shots.

Drop Shot

3 Balls with a lot of back- or top-spin

   To play a drop shot in answer to a ball with heavy spin would require a very strong wrist.

4 Decisive points

   Most players are tense when playing crucial rallies, a bad time to use the drop shot.

5 You are not on form

   If you are not playing your best tennis, your drop shot will be the first to go.

Attacking, Advancing, Playing at the Net

Serving and advancing to the net.

You have two opportunities to move up to the net:

after serving; and
after a short ball.

Toss the ball forwards.

If you want to advance to the net after serving, toss the ball a little further forwards than usual.

If you put all your weight into the ball, you will automatically start forward.

Do not wait for the service to land.

If you have decided to go up to the net, move forward whether the ball lands in the field of play or not.

Serve deep, but not too hard.

The return to a hard service will land in the most unfavourable part of the court — between the base and service lines. However, a long service, hit not too hard, will give you enough time to go forward.

47

Attacking, Advancing, Playing at the Net

Follow the service.

If you serve from point 1A to point 2A and then go up to the net, following the direction of your service, you will be the same distance away from the two possible returns of 2a and 2b.

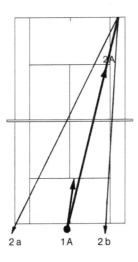

2a   1A   2b

Stop before you volley.

The return must not catch you unawares in the middle of your run. You must interrupt your run to concentrate fully on the ball. Only when your weight is on both feet are you ready to react and move sideways in either direction.

Serving and advancing to the net.

Attacking, Advancing, Playing at the Net

To advance:

you run as fast as possible up to the service line, and

with your last step, you jump into the ready position (see Service return, page 20), your feet about twelve to eighteen inches apart (thirty to forty-five centimetres).

To volley:

from the ready position you do not move parallel to the service line, but forwards, at any angle, towards the ball. This way you reduce the angle of the return.

On your first volley concentrate only on the depth of your shot.

The first volley is not a suitable winning shot. Choosing the angle of the ball involves taking too many risks.

Depth is the best prerequisite for concluding the point with the next volley from the net.

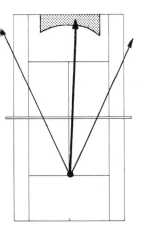

Attacking, Advancing, Playing at the Net

After the first volley, continue up to the net.

Your first, difficult volley has worked. Now is *not* the moment to stand back in the glow of success. *You must hit the second volley from the net.* You can only score at once from there.

2 Attacking a short ball from the net.

Only attack a short ball.

The attack at the net often fails when the player is impatient, because the ball passes him before he has reached the centre of the court.

You can only advance far enough when the *ball is played short,* enabling you to reduce the angle of the return.

Attacking, Advancing, Playing at the Net

Attack deep.

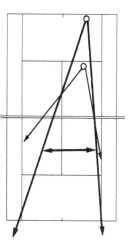

You do not need to play a highly skilled game to attack. A deep ball will do because it

gives you enough time to reach the net, and
reduces the angle of the return.

Once you have decided on your position at the net you must take it up also after too short an attacking shot. In the no-man's-land between base and service line you cannot win.

Be on your guard with short, low shots.

Short, low balls are not as easy to execute as they might seem.

After the moment of contact the ball must rise steeply to cross the net but it must not be hit too hard or it will not land in the field of play.

Remember to

bend your knees;
lift the ball carefully; and
hit it gently.

Attacking, Advancing, Playing at the Net

Attack down the line.

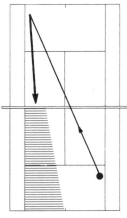

Open court after an
attacking cross ball

The distance to the net is shorter
if you attack down the line.
With a ball hit diagonally across
the court you leave one half of the
court wide open.

This rule is particularly important
when playing a forehand. On the
backhand, an attacking ball played
across court is preferable

if your backhand down the line is
weak; or
if your opponent's backhand is
very weak.

Try a shot down the
centre for a change.

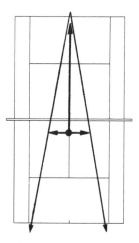

Are you in despair because your
opponent's shots continually pass
you? Then try a shot down the
centre for a change.

He will now have difficulty in
passing you because he cannot
angle his shots so sharply.

The disadvantage of this method of
attack is that your opponent has all
the time in the world to prepare
his shot.

Attacking, Advancing, Playing at the Net

Attacking balls which bounce low reduce the danger of a lobbed return.

If you are afraid of the ball being returned over your head, keep your attacking shots as low as possible. In this way you make it hard for your opponent to use a lob.

Volleying from the ready position.

Whether you follow a service or a short ball to the net you must *interrupt your run to the net in time* to be able to hit the volley from the ready position.

Two other points to remember are:

look only for depth with your first volley; and
keep advancing after the first volley.

3 Net game.

Cover only half the court when at the net.

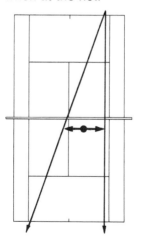

A ball hit diagonally across court from the side line goes over the net in the centre of the court.

If your opponent cannot play very sharply angled shots (particularly rare on the backhand) you need cover only half of the court when you are at the net.

Attacking, Advancing, Playing at the Net

Position yourself exactly between the possible returns.

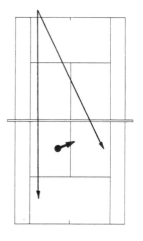

What is true for the game on the baseline is also true for the net game: you should stand in the centre of the possible returns.

In order to know which returns are possible for your opponent, you must be conversant with his repertoire of strokes.

For example, if he has a strongly angled forehand, you must position yourself further to the right than you would usually. This is your only chance of reaching his dangerous crosscourt ball.

On the other hand, you can position yourself further to the left if your opponent has a poor backhand down the line.

Whether you play very close to the net or about two to three yards (two to three metres) away from the net depends on your speed and how highly you rate the danger of a lob.

Do not give up after a weak volley.

A weak volley is no reason to throw in the towel.

If you now concentrate on one side, you have a fifty-fifty chance of reaching your opponent's passing shot — and the odds make the effort worthwhile.

Volley

Push your racket at the ball.

The volley is in no way connected to the ground stroke.

The racket is not swung but *pushed* towards the ball either with a very short backswing or none at all. (Do not draw the racket back behind your shoulders.) The direction the ball takes depends on the direction of the push.

Even gentle volleys should not be hit with a swinging motion or unnecessary mistakes will be made.

Make contact when the ball is still well in front of you.

The secret of a good net player lies in his advancing to the ball to hit it when it is still well in front of him (twelve inches—thirty centimetres —from his body).

Firm wrist.

*This exercise is recommended by Rod Laver.

Is your wrist bent back by the force of the shots that come at you? If so, you should try to iron out this problem by squeezing a tennis ball between your fingers for a while each day.*

To volley well you need a firm wrist.

Volley

Lean forwards towards the ball.

The perfect side-on position to the ball is not absolutely necessary for volleying; indeed you will frequently find you do not have time to take it up.

But you should lean forwards towards the ball whenever possible, to give your volleys the necessary speed and power.

For low volleys bend your knees and slice the ball.

If you keep your legs stiff and your racket face closed your low volleys will frequently land in the net.

Your knees should be bent and *level with the ball* at the moment of contact, often only inches from the ground. The rest of your body should be upright.

As the ball must rise steeply to cross the net, low volleys must be hit *with the racket face open to the ball.*

Volley

Volley shots that come straight at you.

There is no need to be afraid of balls that come straight at you.

Simply move your forearm to the right, so that the racket face comes to rest in front of your body: you can now take the ball comfortably on your backhand.

The drop volley.

The drop shot and drop volley require a very delicate feel for the ball and are not absolutely vital to your repertoire of shots.

The backswing for the drop volley is the same as for a normal volley. After the point of contact, the follow-through is the same as for the drop shot (see page 44).

The low backhand volley.

Half Volley

Only in emergencies.

The half volley requires a delicate touch. If you don't count yourself among the great tennis masters, only use it in emergencies.

Do you often hit half-volleys from the baseline?

If so, then you are either standing too far forward or you are not running back in time to allow the ball to bounce high enough.

Half-volley technique.

Make a note of the following:

use only a very short backswing; bend your knees;

keep your racket open and slice the ball; and

when the ball bounces push your racket towards it.

Like the volley the half volley is played with a punch not with a swing.

Smash

The two stages of the smash.

In contrast to the service, the smash does not consist of one flowing movement. There are two separate actions:

the racket is placed in the ready position behind the head (preparation phase); and
the ball is then smashed from this position (strike phase).

Immediately get *under* the ball.

As soon as you have recognised the shot your opponent is playing, run *under the ball as quickly as possible* as if you wanted to catch it with your left hand. (Many players find the rhythm best to their liking when they stretch their left arm out towards the ball.)

Bring the racket into the waiting position behind your head while you are running.

Draw your racket back as quickly as possible.

The smash is like a *shortened service.* Draw your racket back as rapidly as possible without making a circular movement with your arm.

Smash

The ready position: face the side of the court.

When you are ready to smash the ball the line of your shoulders should be at right angles to the net —as for the service.

Contact with the ball is made directly above your nose.

Smash your racket up at the ball so that the ball is hit directly above your nose; your arm should by now be fully outstretched.

With low lobs contact must naturally be made further in front of you.

Hit the ball gently.

Let your wrist snap forward (as in the service) and you will be astonished how much speed a gentle smash can develop.

Consistency is the first priority with the smash.

Smash

Very high lobs should
be allowed to bounce.

If lobbed, the ball drops almost
vertically and its bounce is difficult
to assess, as a result high lobs
should be allowed to bounce.

The smash.

Doubles

Choosing your partner.

First and foremost choose a partner who has reached the same standard as yourself: two players of average skill will consistently beat a pair made up of a strong opponent and a weak one.

If your game is quite clearly superior to your partner's, you are likely to see the ball so rarely that you will lose interest in the game. On the other hand, if *you* are obviously the weaker player, your partner will lose interest.

Your prospects are especially good if you *complement each other,* for example when:

you have a strong forehand and he has a strong backhand; consistency is your strength and his volleying ability is good; or he is a wily, experienced player who knows all the tricks and you are a good runner with less experience.

Teamwork is based at best on mutual liking and at least respect. If your partner gives vent to his annoyance through grimaces or disparaging comments ('that was an easy ball', 'I see I've got three of you against me today,' etc.), his attitude is hardly likely to bring out the best in you.

Choosing your side.

It is not the strength of your game but your opponent's service return that decides which half of the court you should take.

Doubles

After the service, the forehand volley is the most decisive stroke. Since play down the middle of the court is frequent in doubles, a strong forehand volley has more effect from the left-hand side of the court than from the right.

Long, safe services.

The server should have the two following aims in mind:

to get his opponent to play as high a return as possible; and

to advance as close to the net as possible.

A long service, hit not too hard (with, if possible, some kick or slice) will give the best results.

If you serve very hard the ball comes back before you have reached the service line. Moreover, the risk of a bad shot is much too great and you couldn't give your opponent a more welcome present than a short second service.

Serve on to your opponent's backhand.

In doubles as in singles you should direct most of your services at your opponent's backhand.

Doubles

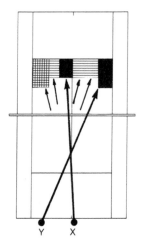

With this aim in view, stand on the right hand side of the court at point X, on the left hand side at point Y.

Occasionally, you can serve to your opponent's forehand (especially from point X) or down the centre of the court, so that your opponent does not have time to prepare for the more frequent shots aimed at his backhand.

Where do you stand when your partner serves?

You should stand approximately half way between the outer sideline and the centre line. You move nearer to the sideline if:

your partner serves from the right hand side of the court on to your opponent's forehand;

your partner's service is too short;

your volleys are noticeably weaker than your partner's; or

you are often passed down the line.

Normally you should stand about two yards (two metres), to be ready for any lobs.

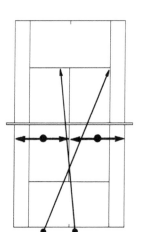

A position behind the baseline is only justified in exceptional circumstances (if, for example, your partner serves very weakly, or has very poor net play).

Doubles

The service return.

The aims of the receiver should
be

to hit the ball past the opposing
net player; and
to keep it as low as possible.

The return should bounce
somewhere along the service line
straight at the feet of an opponent
dashing towards the net. Relatively
soft shots are especially well
suited for the return.
If this shot fails, a lob over the
man at the net is the next best
solution.

Where do you stand
when your partner
returns?

The best place to stand is between
the inner sideline and the centre
line, level with the service line.

From here you should usually be
able to cut off your opposing net
player's volleys, even if your
partner's return is poor.

If you are frequently passed down
the line, you should move your
position a little to the left.

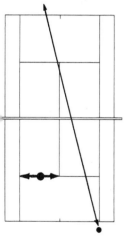

Doubles

Your first priority must be to get close to the net.

Together with your partner, endeavour not only to advance nearer and nearer to the net, but by your own low shots provoke high returns which are fatal to your opponents.

If you serve (or return) and then run up to the net, you must on no account stand still after the first volley, but continue towards your position at the net as quickly as possible.

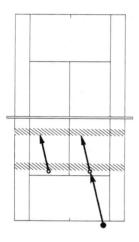

As soon as you are level with your partner, he also runs forward. In this way you form a wall which will be difficult to penetrate. (Your distance from the net should be somewhere between one and three yards (one and three metres) depending on the skill of your opponents.)

When all four players are close to the net.

If you are not close enough to the net to hit the ball down, soft shots played at your opponent's feet will be more effective than hard shots which reach their highest point long after having crossed the net.

Shots which cannot win you the point immediately should be aimed at the player standing further back, whereas with gentle, high volleys you should aim at the nearest player's feet or at his half of the court.

Doubles

If you and your partner are at the net and your opponents are at the back of the court.

To prevent unreachable lobs from passing over your heads, you and your partner should not both be right up at the net.

If the matter has not been prearranged, the player whose head the lobbed ball has passed over should chase after it while his partner runs back from the net. Shots which bounce low reduce the danger of a good lob return.

Move sideways after each shot.

Your position varies according to the direction in which you have just struck the ball.

After a shot aimed at the left hand side of the court (see from your side), you should move to the right in order to stand in the centre of the possible returns.

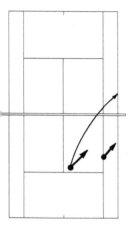

If you are playing from the back and your opponents are at the net.

In this defensive position your objective is to try, with deep shots or lobs, to prevent your opponent striking the ball down when he is right up at the net.

Although the score in a doubles match is, in general, decided by the net positions, clever baseline players can become a dangerous team with these tactics.

Doubles

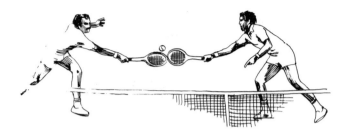

Aim down the middle as often as possible.

Shots aimed down the centre service line are a *very effective weapon* for the following reasons:

the ball cannot go out at the sides; your opponents must stretch just as far as for a shot aimed at the side line;
they will find it difficult to angle the ball; and
they will often be unsure which of them should deal with the shot.

Come to an agreement beforehand.

So that there can be no doubt as to which of you has the task of taking shots played straight down the middle, this point should be settled *before* the contest.

There are three general rules.

Shots played down the centre service line are taken by the player on the left-hand side on his forehand.

Lobs are taken by the man over whose head the ball passes (if both players are at the net).

Lobs which pass over the head of the man at the net are taken by his partner and the two players then swap sides (if one is standing at the net and the other at the baseline). Nevertheless, when the case is debatable, it must be settled as *soon as possible with a clear call.*

Do not always play by the book.

A good net player should always keep his opponent guessing whether he plans to stay in his own court or stray onto his partner's half. The element of surprise will cause his opponent to make many errors, because he will no longer be able to concentrate on the ball, while his attention is diverted to the player at the net.

In this case the winning shot should be attempted when returning a ball played down the centre service line.
When you are 'poaching' your partner's shots avoid offending him:

use a predetermined signal to indicate your intention; and
turn at least fifty per cent of the poached shots into winners.

When playing against a 'poacher' the rules are:

concentrate solely on the ball; and
do not let yourself be diverted from your original intention of playing the ball across court, down the line or over your opponent's head.

69

Doubles

You could also try the Australian doubles position:

If your partner serves from the left hand side, you cover the left side from the net. After serving, your partner runs into the right hand side to take the return. You will thus force your opponent to make his return down the line.

Find out your opponents' weaknesses and make use of them.

Forethought is particularly necessary in doubles. As the match begins to warm up you and your partner should consider the following questions and answers.

Is the ball frequently passing over our heads? Then don't advance too close to the net.

Do one, or both opponents always reply to certain shots with a lob? Then be prepared for it in plenty of time.

Do they always play close to the net? Occasional lobs will force them back.

Do they leave a lot of room down the middle? Play down the middle on important points.

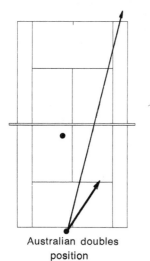

Australian doubles position

Which of our opponents has a poor volley or smash? Play to him more often when he is at the net.

Which of our opponents is weaker down the baseline? Adjust your game to this.

Do our opponents serve or return according to a set pattern? Then you know right from the start where to position yourselves.

Training

Assessing Your Weaknesses

The standard method of training will not get you very far.

Compared with other sportsmen, most tennis players have a remarkably casual attitude to training.

To most, training consists of warming up for about ten minutes, hammering a few test services over the net and then starting a contest which they play as they would a competition match (except that they are under less pressure). There are also people who simply play the ball back and forth for hours, shunning all possible competition.

With that sort of training you might just be able to maintain your level.

Your aim:

to strengthen your game a little with every hour of training, will only be attained with a *systematic approach*.

Personal assessment.

The main factors which determine a player's strength are listed in the section 'Playing'. They have been carried over (point for point and in the same order as in the text) into the *check list* below.

To work out which should be your priorities in training go through each section and ask yourself:

Should I make a special note of this point or simply bear it in mind?

Assessing Your Weaknesses

Make a tick in the appropriate box marked:

important or very important.

In the adjacent column headed 'Notes' indicate those points which are of special importance to you (the various points made in the book are listed in the check list).

For example:

Section	Page	Rating		Notes
		important	very important	
Service Return: ready position.	14	☐	☒	Weight on the balls of the feet

Mundane as the task may seem do not give up; the results will be very helpful and there are ways of simplifying your task:

ask a friend to watch you playing and to make a note of your weaknesses; or

even better, if you can get hold of a cine camera, ask someone to film you in action.

Once you have completed the chart you can enter the improvements you make as you go along.

Assessing Your Weaknesses

A great help in training
and competition.

With the chart you have not just a
basis for your future training. You
can skim through the check list
before a match and make a note
again of two or three (but no more)
of the most important points.

You will be astonished how much
success this will bring you.

Personal Assessment

Section	Page	Rating		Notes
		important	very important	
Concentration and Relaxing	9			
Concentrating on the ball.	9			
Billie Jean King's concentration exercise	10			
Concentrating on your opponent and the game.	10			
Running and Positioning	11			
React in plenty of time.	11			
Standing to receive the ball.	11			
Retreating when the opponent plays a deep return.	12			
After the shot go straight back to the centre of the possible returns.	12			
Serving	13			
Seventy per cent of your first services should go into the service box.	14			
Avoid a second service in crucial situations.	14			
Play to your opponent's backhand, but not all the time.	14			
Vary spin and speed whenever possible.	15			
Depth of your second service.	15			
Relax!	16			
Begin slowly.	16			
Correct stance.	16			

Correct toss. 17
Throw the racket head up to the ball. 18
Hit the ball when it is at its highest
  position. 18
Snap with your wrist. 18
Weight transference. 19

Service return 20

The ready position. 20
Concentrate on the ball. 21
Begin your backswing as early as
  possible. 21
Short backswing. 21
Shoulder pointing at the net. 21
'Attack' the ball and hit it when it is still
  in front of your body. 22
Watch your opponent toss the ball. 22
Returning a hard service:
  stand back far enough, put weight in to
  the ball. 23
Returning a kick service:
  take the ball as it rises and 'attack' it. 24
Returning a slice service:
  don't stand too far back, advance
  diagonally to take the ball. 24
If your opponent stays on the baseline
  after serving make a deep return. 25
If your opponent advances after serving:
  concentrate on the ball, not on your
  opponent. 25
try to keep the return low. 26
don't always play to his left or right; aim
  straight at him as well, or, occasionally, over his head. 26

Personal Assessment

Section	Page	Rating		Notes
		important	very important	
Passing shot	27			
The three basic rules:				
1 Keep your eyes only on the ball.	27			
2 Keep the ball low.	27			
3 Play straight at him occasionally.	27			
Never try a passing shot when hard-pressed: lob instead.	27			
Playing from the baseline	28			
Consistency.	28			
Depth.	28			
Play the ball high enough over the net.	28			
After each shot, get back to the centre of any possible returns.	29			
After a shot played down the line you must run parallel to the baseline *beyond* the centre mark.	30			
After a crosscourt shot, stop *before* the centre mark.	30			
The centre depends also on your opponent.	31			
The crosscourt shot is easier and safer than the shot played down the line.	32			
Occasionally play a ball short and across court.	32			
When under pressure play high.	33			

Forehand and Backhand   34

Swing back early.   34
Backswing on the run.   35
Short backswing.   35
As little wrist action as possible.   36
The line of your shoulders should be at
     right angles to the net.   36
Attack the ball.   36
Put the weight of your body into the ball.   37
Point of contact in front of you.   37
Follow the stroke through.   38
Stay where you are.   38

Lob   40

The shot when you are hard-pressed.   40
The lob as a rhythm breaker.   41
The lob as a substitute for a passing
     shot.   41
Follow your lob to the net.   42
Lobbing into the sun.   42
Play high lobs deep enough.   42
Aim at your opponent's backhand.   43
Long, upward follow-through.   43
Only for the real experts: the attacking
     lob.   43

Personal Assessment

Section	Page	Rating		Notes
		important	very important	
Drop shot				
The racket face is placed under the ball.	44			
Hit the ball when it is still well in front of you.	44			
Pretend to hit a ground stroke.	44			
Don't consider the point won too soon.	44			
The drop shot as an attacking shot.	45			
Situations unsuited to the drop shot:	45			
deep shots;	45			
hard shots;	45			
balls with a lot of back- or top-spin;	45			
decisive points;	46			
you are not on form.	46			
Attacking, advancing, playing at the net	47			
1 Serving and advancing to the net.	47			
Toss the ball forwards.	47			
Do not wait for the service to land.	47			
Serve deep, but not too hard.	47			
Follow the service.	48			
Stop before you volley.	48			
On your first volley concentrate only on the depth of your shot.	49			
After the first volley, continue up to the net.	50			

2 Attacking a short ball from the net 50
Only attack a short ball. 50
Attack deep. 51
Be on your guard with short, low shots. 51
Attack down the line. 52
Try a shot down the centre for a
   change. 52
Attacking balls which bounce low
   reduce the danger of a lobbed
   return. 53
Volleying from the ready position. 53
Look only for depth with your first
   volley. 53
Keep advancing after the first volley. 53

3 Net game 53
Cover only half the court when at the
   net. 53
Position yourself exactly between the
   possible returns. 54
Do not give up after a weak volley. 54

Volley 55

Push your racket at the ball. 55
Make contact when the ball is still well
   in front of you. 55
Firm wrist. 55
Lean forwards towards the ball. 56
For low volleys bend your knees and
   slice the ball. 56
Volley shots that come straight at you. 57
The drop volley. 57

Personal Assessment

Section	Page	Rating		Notes
		important	very important	
Half volley	58			
Only in emergencies.	58			
Very short backswing.	58			
Bend your knees.	58			
Racket face open, slice the ball.	58			
When the ball bounces, push your racket	58			
towards it.	59			
Smash	59			
The two stages of the smash:				
The racket is placed in the ready				
position behind the head; and				
the ball is then smashed from this	59			
position.				
Immediately get under the ball.	59			
Draw your racket back as quickly as				
possible.	60			
The ready position: face the side of				
the court.	60			
Contact with the ball is made directly	60			
above your nose; low lobs are hit				
further forward.	61			
Hit the ball gently.				
Very high lobs should be allowed to				
bounce.				

Working on Your Weaknesses

Consistency is the key to good tennis.

You have by now made a mental note of the areas in which some improvement will be necessary.

If you now stay the course and work systematically on your weaknesses, you cannot fail to improve your game. Hitting the ball onto your opponent's court is the top priority in tennis. This apparent truism is too often forgotten, if not in competitions, at least in training.

The result of inconsistent training is inconsistent tennis.

Training methods.

There are four methods of training using

training exercises (with a partner);
a training wall;
an automatic ball machine; or
playing a
practice match.

A good training programme would include half-an-hour of training exercises (using a training wall or an automatic ball machine), and a half-hour practice match.

Do not underestimate the value of the practice match. Otherwise you will develop into a training player and not a match player.

Working on Your Weaknesses

Which of the first three training methods you choose will obviously depend on the facilities available to you.

Training with a partner.

Begin with exercise 1 or 2 to find your rhythm. Then select those exercises which you (and your partner) really need. Remember your priorities:

consistency;
depth;
accuracy; and
speed.

1 Getting the feel of the ball.

Both players stand on the service line and play soft shots which bounce between two and five yards (two and five metres) beyond the net.

As both get a better feel of the ball, they slowly retire towards the baseline.

2 Consistency.

The players stand on their respective baselines and each tries to trap his opponent into making a mistake.

Players with some experience can put their opponents under pressure with depth, accuracy, variety of shots and well-planned attacks at the net, but even here emphasis is laid on consistency.

The winner of the rally scores a point, and the first to score 20 wins the 'game'.

Working on Your Weaknesses

Depth.

The players stand well back. Both must play shots that, at the very least, cross the service line before bouncing. Later on, an imaginary line is drawn about three yards (three metres) in front of the baseline and this must be crossed.

Here again, mock 'games' can be played.

Accuracy.

Both players stand well back and exchange shots, first forehand, then backhand, crosscourt and down the line respectively, the latter being practised most frequently since it is the more difficult of the two shots.

Remember to run back to your initial position after each shot.

Exercises 3 and 4 can be combined.

Serving and advancing to the net.

Player A places his service deep on to his opponent's backhand and goes up to the net.

Player B endeavours to hit the ball, so that A can hit a long volley first time from along the service line.

A wins a point when B misses his return.

Working on Your Weaknesses

B gets a point when A

doesn't get his service into the field
of play;
misses the volley; or
hits the volley too short, i.e., not
beyond the service line.

6 Attacking on a short
ball.

Each player tries, using long shots
to trap his opponent into playing a
short ball. He then attacks down
the line and finishes off at the net.

The winner of each rally scores
one point.

7 Volleying from the
centre of the court.

Player B stands well back.

A takes up a position along the
service line and returns B's shots
(hit as consistently as possible)
with long volleys or half-volleys.

8 Volleys and half-
volleys.

a) The players stand on their
respective lines and volley.

Start slowly, then step up the
pace.

Working on Your Weaknesses

b) The players stand one or two yards (one or two metres) in front of the baseline, begin with slow volleys, and gradually work their way to the net.

Again start slowly, then step up the pace.

c) Player A stands at the net and volleys. To test the speed of his reactions, B hits five shots at him in quick succession from the service line.

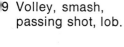

9 Volley, smash, passing shot, lob.

Player A stands about two yards (two metres) away from the net and volleys or smashes, *immediately* reassuming his initial position after each shot.

B plays alternate passing shots and lobs.

To make this kind of rally possible, A must not hit his volleys and smashes too hard or out of reach of B's racket.

Working on Your Weaknesses

10 Running and fitness.

a) Both players stand well back. A plays crosscourt, B plays down the line.

Try to achieve a regular, moderately paced rhythm.

b) Player B stands at the net and volleys alternately on to A's forehand and backhand.

A runs from side to side at the back and plays the balls back to B.

Using a training wall.

Do you dislike playing against the wall because the balls come back erratically and too quickly for any real game to develop?

If so, it is highly likely that your shots land just as erratically when you are training with a partner on a proper court.

Meanwhile, you should only make use of a training wall if you have no one to play with.

If you start slowly and hit gentle shots aimed one or two yards over the imaginary net line, you will gradually get a feel for the balls.

Almost all shots can be practised against a wall. The smash, in particular, is easy to adapt; the ball should bounce just short of the wall so that it returns as a lob.

The wall is also excellent for warming up before a match.

Working on Your Weaknesses

Using an automatic ball machine.

In the USA and Australia (the two countries which have so far produced the majority of the world's top-class players) the value of training with an automatic ball machine has long been recognised. Tennis coaches there use the machines to analyse the weaknesses of their pupils without the pupils' attention being distracted; and, the machine is especially useful in group coaching.

If this valuable training machine were at your disposal, your main problem as a beginner of finding a consistent training partner, would be solved.

To get the best use out of the machine, four players can take part in any training session. While two players hit between twenty and twenty-five balls per minute, the other two collect the balls. Then the two pairs swap rôles.

Modern automatic ball machines can be set to produce all possible rally combinations (e.g., a long ball, a stop ball and a lob) and they are easy to operate.

Working on Your Weaknesses

Playing a practice match.

Most players tend not to differentiate between a tournament and a practice match: in both they concentrate overmuch on the task of winning.

This should not be the main aim of the training session which is designed to help players work on their weak points.

If your backhand is poor, this is not the moment to run round the ball to play a forehand. You must not be afraid of mishits or of losing points; on the contrary you should play those very shots which you feel uneasy about.

Winning a training session must be seen as a secondary aim. If you are running round the ball to play a forehand you must change your attitude. All the self-discipline you have in training will be more than repaid by an increased number of victories in tournaments.

Competition Training

The technical aspect.

There are two sides to training: the technical and the competitive.

The technical side has been dealt with extensively in the previous chapter. All that remains to be said is that in competition training you must take into consideration the conditions which are peculiar to the competition itself.

You must therefore:

train against several partners to learn how to adjust to different methods of play (here weaker players can also be helpful).

train at the same hour (e.g., early in the morning) as you will probably have to compete;

train longer than usual, to prepare for a long match;

train under unfavourable weather and court conditions;

occasionally use your second racket, so that you are familiar with it; and

use the make of ball which will be used in the competition.

The competitive aspect.

To win in competition, a general knowledge of tactics and psychology is indispensable.

Competition Training

Although the importance of the latter is not disputed, it is amazing how little attention the average tennis player (and his coach) pays to this aspect of the game.

Yet, with relatively little trouble, you could acquire a knowledge of tactics and psychology which would considerably improve your game in competitions.

Mental Training and Learning by Spectating

What is mental training?

Mental training involves actually memorizing a particular series of movements so as to be able to reproduce it on the tennis court.

The USA has been using mental training for years with astonishing success. The following experiment illustrates better than any long-winded explanation could what the term means and what the method can achieve:

The members of three US basket-ball teams were asked to prepare, over a period of about four months, for a test of free throws (throws at the basket from a distance of about five yards—five metres). Each team used a different method of training:

The first team had throwing practice daily in the gymnasium;
The second team underwent daily mental training, during which the members drew an exact mental picture of the throw technique and of successful shots;
The third team had no training at all.

As expected, the third team made no improvement, the first team increased its hitting quota by ninety-eight per cent, *the second team improved by ninety-six per cent!*

To be as successful as that, mental training must of course, be practised with at least as much concentration as normal training on the court.

Mental Training and Learning by Spectating

Mental training, immediately befor
or even during a competition (whe
changing sides), is becoming
increasingly popular in tennis. Its
supporters are convinced that the
mental picture is not only beneficia
to their shots, but also does their
nerves good.

Learning by spectating.

Learning by spectating is closely
connected with mental training.
The successes of a great number
of former world-class players who
began as ball boys, have their root
in this method.

Naturally, to learn, you need to
concentrate on one particular
aspect or shot at a time. Showing
a general interest in the game of a
professional will not particularly
help your game.
You will profit most from spectatin
if you try to put your observations
into practice without delay.

itness

the importance of fitness.

It has long been recognised that someone who is fit has many advantages over someone who is not:

he is better equipped against premature ageing, obesity, diabetes, back ailments and diseases of the heart and circulatory system;

he is in a better position to deal with both physical and mental stress; and

in general, he is more relaxed. So keep fit!

When he is playing crucial points, the fit tennis player is able to mobilize his physical and psychological reserves

to run fast;

to concentrate on the ball;

to think, analyse; and

to fight,

when physical strength, concentration, mental powers and fighting spirit have long since flagged in the unfit player.

The tennis player with stamina knows that even when conditions are unfavourable (e.g., when his form is poor), he will be capable of putting up a good fight. This knowledge gives him *self-confidence* which, in turn, strengthens his fighting spirit.

Fitness

Make use of every
opportunity.

If it is impossible for you to follow
a regular training programme, you
should at least alter certain habits
in your daily life with the aim of
improving your physical condition,
for example,

instead of strolling, walk fast or run

cover short stretches on foot
instead of by car or by bus;

use the stairs instead of the
elevator.

When you are walking, swimming
or skiing,

walk as fast as possible for five or
ten minutes;

swim 200 yards (183 m) as fast as
you can; or

ski down a long slope without
stopping.

itness

When you fully appreciate the
advantages of good physical fitness
for your personal sense of well-
being and your tennis, you will no
longer be satisfied with less than

ten or fifteen minutes training daily,
or
one or two hours' training weekly.

The following training programme
is designed to suit the special
requirements of tennis. (The
exercises are selected from ones
which you will doubtless recognise
at once.) As your physical fitness
gradually improves so should the
speed with which you do those
exercises. Try to take *as few breaks
as possible.* Don't stop as soon as
you begin to feel tired. It can only
do a healthy person good to get
close to the limits of his endurance.

eg exercises.
Pick out one of the four
rogrammes).

1 Running on the spot.

Simulate the running motion, but
keep your toes on the ground.

Crouch down slowly so that you
rest your behind on your heels,
rise, and start again.

Jump up and make a rapid
scissor motion in the air with
your legs.

Simulate the Cossack dance,
keeping your arms folded in front
of your body.

Fitness

2 Jump

on the spot, first legs together and then hopping;

forwards, backwards, sideways, turning in the air;

on the spot in a squatting position;

forwards in a squatting position.

3 Skip

legs together;

on one leg;

forwards and backwards;

while running on the spot;

in a squatting position, with a shortened rope.

4 Run

five or ten yard (five or ten metres) sprinting and finish off over ten or twenty yards(ten or twenty metres);

backwards and sideways;
in a zigzag (slalom);

long distances (440 yards, one mile, two miles—400 m, $\frac{1}{2}$ km, 2 km).

Exercises for the arms, shoulders and spine.

Draw large, full circles with your arms.

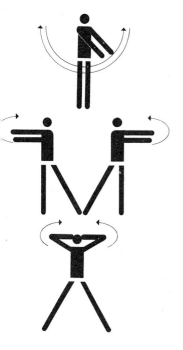

Swing your arms from side to side (see illustration).

Your hands clasped together and your arms held out horizontally in front of your body, swing your arms round to your left and then to your right.

Do press-ups.

With your hands clasped together behind your neck, swing your body round alternately to the left and to the right (see illustration).

Lying on your stomach with your arms stretched out at the sides, raise your chest, arms and legs.

xercises for the neck.

Describe circles with your head. Rock your head back and forth.

xercise for the wrist.

Squeeze a ball hard between your fingers.

xercises for the spine, nd stomach.

With your feet apart and your arms stretched straight above your head, bend at the waist and touch the ground with the palms of your hands.

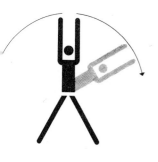

From the same position, bend to either side of your body.

With your feet apart and your hands on your hips, describe large circles with your body, first in a clockwise, then in an anti-clockwise direction.

Fitness

Lie on your back, with your hands clasped behind your neck: gently raise your legs off the floor and cross them.

Lie on your back with your arms stretched out above your head: raise your back and touch your toes with your finger tips (see illustration).

Lie on your back, with your arms stretched out above your head: simultaneously raise your chest, arms and legs (the jackknife, see illustration).

Lie on your back, with your hands clasped behind your neck and you legs stretched straight upwards: bicycle with your legs.

Winning

he little things that count

It is not worth losing an important game just because:

you weren't awake when the match started; or

you went on court on a full stomach; or

you went on court in an agitated state; or

you feel stiff; or

you haven't got a good spare racket; or

you've forgotten your tennis shoes!

To avoid making unnecessary problems for yourself, select your equipment carefully.

quipment.

The best idea is to get used to having too much rather than too little. After a short break it can be thoroughly unpleasant to have to play in the same old sweaty shirt. In warm weather you will need a change of kit; in cold weather you will need extra warm clothing.

At least two days before the start of any competition, you should check over your rackets, shoes and kit to make sure that you have all you need and that it is all in good condition. If anything is missing, you will then have plenty of time to see to it.

The little things that count

The things you almost always need and those you might need are separately listed below. The blank space is provided in case there are any items that you personally consider essential.

essential	optional
tennis bag	bag for dirty clothes
racket, spare racket	racket for bad weather
shoes	spare shoes
socks, spare socks	shoe laces
shorts, skirt(s), tennis dress(es)	track suit
	sweat bands
shirt, spare shirt(s)	handkerchief
sweater, jacket	wrist band
underwear	sun-hat, head band
towel(s)	balls for warming up
soap, shampoo, etc.	something to drink
sticking plasters (for blisters)	glucose tablets
	sawdust or resin (to stop your hands getting sweaty)
	sports spectacles
	talcum powder, foot spray

Get up in plenty of time.

Even if your game is set for early morning you must be up two or three hours before it begins, because your body needs a lot of time to wake up. Many tournament players feel alert only after a ten or fifteen minute run.

The little things that count

If you cannot adapt to getting up early, it would be a good idea occasionally to have your training sessions in the early hours of the morning.

No late, greasy meals.

About one and a half or two hours before the game you should have a meal which is high neither in fat nor in starch content. Recommended are meat, salads and fruit. Do not drink too much milk.

Don't rush.

Having to hurry will contribute to your tension. You should arrive at the courts in good time to prepare for the game.

Limbering-up exercises.

Many players fall behind right at the start of the match because they are still cold and their muscles are stiff.

If you have no intention of handing the first game to your opponent on a plate, and you want to avoid pulled muscles, try the following limbering-up exercises:

stretch your arms as high as possible then bend down slowly to touch the ground with your hands;

gently, bend your knees, straighten up again;

describe circles with your head, arms and hands;

briefly stand on tip-toes, resume normal position, repeat.

The little things that count

Warming up.

Like the limbering-up exercises, warming-up is an essential part of the tournament player's preparation. You should pay special attention to all those strokes that you usually have trouble with at the start of the game, the service, volley, smash, lob, etc.

The time needed to warm up varies from person to person. Should you be one of these players who need a long time to get into their stride, you must make the necessary allowance for time.

Overcome nervousness, adopt a positive attitude

Apprehension.

Many players are already beaten before the match even starts simply because of their apprehension.

Instead of looking forward to the contest, their attitude is characterized by fear:

fear of losing,

fear of playing badly,

fear of not doing themselves justice,

fear of disappointing their team, friends or relatives, or

fear of making fools of themselves.

Before the game this uneasiness manifests itself by irritability, listlessness or even the wish to not appear on court at all.

During the game they feel paralysed. Legs and arms are like lead, breathing is short, strokes are tense and abrupt; their game is uncontrolled or overcautious, their spirits are low.

How to overcome nervousness before the game.

An excellent method of overcoming nervousness is to brainwash yourself into underestimating the importance of playing a good or bad game.

In actual fact, even the most shameful defeat is hardly going to rock the world to its foundations. It will be forgotten much sooner than you think.

Overcome nervousness, adopt a positive attitude

No match, however important, is worth being frightened about.

Conquering your nerves during the game.

Bad attacks of nerves can become a serious handicap, especially on decisive points. Fear of having victory snatched from you at the last moment leads to tension. To avoid this, you should:

breath out deeply;

give yourself plenty of time between the points and before each service;

hold your racket loosely;

relax your legs, arms, fingers and neck muscles;

concentrate solely on the ball; and, follow the ball through well.

Slight attacks of nerves are normal.

Results of a survey revealed that over ninety per cent of top-class players have to fight with their nerves. Slight nervousness is, in fact, not only normal but even a prerequisite. It contributes to your concentration because, while you are worried, you will be able to think only about the game.

How a nervous person reacts.

But during a *bad* attack of nerves, your fighting spirit is paralyzed, defeat seems inevitable. To be well insured against this

some people react by having every conceivable excuse lined up before the game, or by looking for something else to blame during the game, the umpire, balls, court, etc.;

Overcome nervousness, adopt a positive attitude

others react by taking shelter behind their tension. They place the onus for their poor play on their nervousness instead of on themselves.

Thorough preparation is the basis of a positive attitude.

The prerequisite for a positive, competitive attitude is thorough preparation. The certainty,

of being in good physical shape;

of knowing the most important tactics;

of knowing your own and, if possible, your opponent's strengths and weaknesses and being able to make corresponding adjustments;

of having trained sensibly; and

of having paid attention to every detail during training;

will give you the comforting feeling of having prepared in every way for the challenge.

Healthy self-assessment.

You will spare yourself many bitter disappointments if you take only your *average* training form as a guide to the performance you will achieve in the tournament.

It is unrealistic to imagine that your competition performance will match the top performance you achieve perhaps once or twice a year.

Overcome nervousness, adopt a positive attitude

Over-rating your own ability will not necessarily have an unfavourable effect on your competition performance, but it will certainly make you personally disappointed.

Extremely bad competition players are those who *under-rate* their chances to insure themselves against possible defeat (which then generally ensues). They fail at the decisive moment because they have no faith in themselves. Despite their stock of excuses they will be disappointed.

Don't allow anyone to shake your self-confidence.

Even if you do not suffer from a lack of self-confidence, a comment made shortly before the game could give you a jolt that could weaken your tennis at the decisive moment. Therefore:

avoid discussions about the coming game with your opponent or with outsiders;

ignore your opponent's record and other people's talk about the power of his play: base your opinions solely on your own observations;

even the best player has his weaknesses so try to find out what they are as early on as possible; they will reassure you; and

look forward to the contest as a challenge, to be taken up and dealt with as well as possible.

Overcome nervousness, adopt a positive attitude

You can't give any more than your best.

A positive attitude to competition consists of wanting to give no more and no less than one's best. Even if you are not on your best form, you should remember not to lose heart and to fight to the last. If your favourite shot suddenly goes, forget it and try out an alternative.

A positive attitude always pays. If your opponent beats you, there is no point in being disappointed when you have given your best and nobody, not even you, can demand more of you. In fact, if you adopt that attitude, you have excellent prospects of winning.

Knowing Yourself and Your Opponent

Your ability determines your tactics.

It is no use knowing that a certain tactic exists if you haven't mastered the necessary technique.

What use are drop shots which constantly land in the net, even if your opponent runs slowly? What is the point of wanting to play on to a left-hander's weak backhand, if you cannot play backhands down the line?

A knowledge of your own strengths and weaknesses should dictate your strategy.

You do not need to have mastered every shot to win. Even without drop shots and backhand shots down the line you can play a good game.

Make full use of your strengths to compensate for your weaknesses.

During your training you have concentrated on ironing out your weaknesses.

In competition you should make full use of your strengths to compensate for your weaknesses.

When applied to the example mentioned in the previous paragraph, this means:

you do without drop shots, instead you make your opponent chase back and forth; or, using only your forehand, you play onto his weak backhand.

There are a host of such compensatory possibilities:

Knowing Yourself and Your Opponent

Weakness	Compensation
Second service	Get ninety per cent of your first services into the service box.
Backhand	Play safely. If the opportunity presents itself run round the ball.
Service return, when your opponent advances to the net	Dont attempt to accurately place the ball, just aim it straight at him or lob.
Passing shot	Lob or hit soft balls at your opponent's feet.
Drop shot	Outmanoeuvre your opponent with long shots or with short, angled forehand cross-court shots.

Know your opponent.

The second essential aspect to be taken into consideration when planning your strategy, is the sum of your opponent's strengths and weaknesses. This requirement, which is already taken for granted in other competitive sports, is too often ignored in tennis.

However, a detailed knowledge of the opponent's game has, again and again, been the decisive factor (remember the Wimbledon final of 1975 between Ashe and Connors).

Knowing Yourself and Your Opponent

Study your opponent
before the match.

If it is at all possible you should analyse your opponent's game before the match. You can then plan your strategy without having to hurry.

If you are unable to watch him *before* the match, you should use the warming up period and, if possible, the first games to make a careful assessment of his strengths and weaknesses.

What type of player
is he?

In all likelihood you will be able to assign your opponent to one of these nine categories:

1 He has an especially powerful shot.

2 He has an obvious weakness.

3 He makes many unnecessary mistakes; he 'hammers' the ball.

4 He volleys at the net.

5 He returns everything.

6 He puts backspin or topspin on everything.

7 He is the better player.

8 He is left-handed.

9 His game has no special features.

The following pages explain how to deal with a player who falls into one of these categories.

He has an especially
powerful shot.

a) Service

Your positioning depends on the
the speed and spin of his service.
If he serves very hard, but with no
spin, you can easily take up a
a position about two yards (two
metres) behind the baseline.

To receive a slice or kick service,
you should stand close to the
baseline. In most cases you can
recognise such a service by the
toss of the ball (slice: from your
vantage point to the left, kick:
from your vantage point to the
right) and you can position yourself accordingly.

If he does not follow his service
to the net, your best shot is a long,
high ball that gives you time to
return to the centre of the possible
returns.

If he advances to the net after
serving, you must keep your
returns low. You achieve this by
blocking off the ball with as short
a backswing as possible so that
the ball bounces along the service
line. The best solution of all is to
aim your returns at his feet and
occasionally throw in a lob to
make him lose his rhythm.

b) Fore- or backhand
strength

If you constantly try to play onto
his weaker side, he will transfer
his initial position more and more
to that half and you will be forced
to place your shots nearer and
nearer to the sideline, at the risk
of playing the ball out of court.

Concentrate on the depth rather than the direction of your shots.

Scoring points directly from the back will be hard for him if you search out the centre of the possible returns immediately after each stroke. You may have to position yourself a little further back than usual. If so, you can attack his balls instead of being overwhelmed by them.

When the conditions are favourable, try to catch him on his *strong side.* In doing so, you open up the whole court and force him to relinquish his tried and tested pattern (running round the weak shot, until you play too short or out at the side). Hit as you run: his return will surely turn out harmless. Players with strong top-spin in particular do not like having to stretch.

You should *vary the direction of your shots* if possible so that he cannot focus on one half of the court from the very start. Concentrate on your first service. He will ruthlessly convert short second services into points for himself.

If you have the necessary qualifications, *attack* is the best form of defence. Concentrate at first on the depth of your shots and, if he repeatedly passes you, try shots down the centre service line. He will not find it quite so easy to pass you, even with his strong shot.

He has an obvious
weakness.

a) Service

Do not be misled by his first
service. It is probably an ace which
only has a success rate of about
ten per cent. It is now up to you to
cash in on his short, and therefore
weak, second service. There are
five alternatives:

Stand far enough forward.
(Occasionally you can stand too
far forward, to force him into
making a double fault.)

Concentrate on the ball as much
as possible.

Don't hit the ball as hard as if you
were standing behind the baseline.

Run round your (weaker) backhand while in the right hand side
of court. (In the left hand side of
court this manoeuvre is perilous
because you leave the whole court
undefended.)

Attack mostly his backhand and
then advance to the net.

b) Fore- or backhand
weakness

There are three ways of dealing
with such an opponent.

1 Play on to his weak side, until it
collapses.

2 At the first opportunity play on
   to his *stronger side* (here
   sharply-angled crosscourt shots
   would be very appropriate). This
   forces him to reveal his weak
   shot, which he now has to make
   use of from a difficult position.

3 You play as if he didn't have any
   weakness at all, and you *only*
   attack this weakness *on
   important points*.

Which of the three alternatives
you decide on depends on your
opponent's play and on your ability

The first and most common method
is only effective under the following
conditions:

you can play onto his weak side
from every position; and

he doesn't run round your shots.

Even if these prerequisites apply,
you should not play a whole match
blindly to this plan, but ask yourself
from time to time whether it is
working. The stroke played
hesitantly at the start could turn
into a reliable weapon if you
constantly force him to practise it
during the match.

The second and third methods do
not have the same disadvantage.

Moreover:
they presuppose less technical
skill, thereby reducing your margin
of errors;

Nine different players and how to play against them

they make it difficult for your opponent to run round his weak side; and

they include an element of surprise.

Players with a weak forehand or backhand frequently begin their backswing too late and hit the ball much too late. The quickest way to get to grips with them is to use long, powerful shots.

Others do not like having to work to keep the ball moving. Use soft, high shots against them.

c) Weakness at the net

The player who is weak at the net dispenses with volleys and smashes while warming up and, even on occasions most suited to attacking, he edges back instead of moving to the net.

Cashing in on this weakness is not quite so simple as it sounds. In fact, your only change is to force him towards the net with drop shots; this done, you can't fail to win the point. (If he falls back, play a passing shot aimed straight at him; if he stays at the net, play a lob.)

The success of his method depends on your proficiency in using drop shots at the right moment and at disguising them well. On no account should you overdo it. He will eventually adjust to your game and you will lose your rhythm.

119

Nine different players and how to play against them

d) Poor footwork

Most players in this category have particular trouble with running forwards and backwards. It is therefore worth making them run from side to side and, occasionally, back and forth. If you have not mastered the drop shot the only alternative is the lob.

If your opponent tires quickly, you should force him to do a lot of running from the start. Even if you make mistakes in doing so, even if you lose the first set, this tactic will bring its rewards later.

Playing two consecutive shots into the same corner is not recommended against tired players. As they have no strength left to run back to the centre of the possible returns, they will be in just the right position.

e) Lack of imagination

Your great advantage will consist in recognising his simple plan quickly and adjusting your game to it as soon as possible. You will then know where his shot must land even before he has started his backswing.

Lobbing will not occur to him, so you can advance close to the net.

Should he try a drop shot, he will give away his intention very early.

The unimaginative player can have his concentration thoroughly ruined by a varied style of play. If you throw in dinks or very high lobs he will make the silliest

mistakes and work himself up
into a real fury over it. As a result
half the battle will be won.

3 He makes many
unnecessary mistakes;
he 'hammers' the ball.

Such a player has no control over
his shots and will make a great
many errors when playing simple
shots.

Your mistake would be to try and
keep up the same pace as him
instead of concentrating on safe
shots.

Don't be put off by a succession of
lucky shots. Position yourself a
yard further back than usual to
attack sharp balls. You may get
little applause with your style of
play, but you will have a lot of
success.

4 He volleys at the net.

Players who attack at the net are
dangerous because they trap their
opponent into making hasty returns
and thus many mishits. If they
constantly stay at the net, they can
make their opponents feel
inescapably hemmed in.

You can prevent the effect of such
a threat in two ways:

a) Skilful defence

You should devote the *whole* of
your attention solely to the ball
and pay no attention at all to
your opponent.

121

Your service returns and passing shots should

be kept low, and

be varied; e.g., aim the shots at him or over him.

He probably volleys well because he advances very close to the net. If you don't throw in any lobs, he will be able to hit down even your lowest passing shots.

At this point, you should recall a rule which is all too often ignored: *when hard-pressed a high lob is by far the best defensive shot.*

If even on your service he advances to the net, you should direct your service at the sideline. This way you lengthen his path to the net.

b) Attacking yourself

Naturally, this tactic only works if your volleys are up to scratch. By storming the net at every suitable opportunity, you rob him of the initiative and *impose your game on him.*

Your chances of success are good because:

you take him by surprise with this method; and

he is certainly not as strong when he is on the defensive as when he is on the offensive.

Nine different players and how to play against them

5 He returns everything.

His greatest strengths are a fighting spirit, running and concentration. They mark him as an opponent to be taken seriously, a player who is always capable of surprising you.

The greatest favour you can do him is to underestimate his ability and to try to sweep him off the court. He will react with indifference to the few points that you score directly, whereas you will get more and more annoyed about your own faults until you end up beating yourself.

Prepare yourself for a difficult match. *You must play him for every point.* To stay the course for a whole match, you need:

1 *Patience:* you must wait until you get a favourable opportunity to attack (e.g., after his short balls). If his shots have plenty of depth, you have no option but to join in the endless rallies.

2 *Concentration:* you can only beat him if you don't make any unnecessary mistakes. This means paying special attention to even simple balls.

3 *Thought:* you should consider from time to time whether your tactics are having the desired effect.

Nine different players and how to play against them

Consider the following situations which might develop against such a player:

a) *You attack: he passes you every time:*

Are your attacking shots deep enough?
Are your attacks mostly aimed down the line?
Have you forced the pace on your first volley, rather than looking only for depth?
Did you stand still after your first volley instead of advancing?
Are you standing in the centre of the possible returns?
Can you not reduce the angle of his returns by attacking down the centre service line?

b) *You attack; he plays over your head every time:*

Are you getting under the ball soon enough?
Are you not positioned too far forward?
How does he react to low, attacking shots played into the half court? (It is difficult to play a good lob from this position).

c) *You play from the back; he simply doesn't put a foot wrong:*

Shouldn't you bring him to the net now and then, and play over his head? (He may not be a good net player.

Nine different players and how to play against them

Can you tire him out, to profit from his mistakes later on? (A tired player usually loses some of his consistency).

If nothing helps and you lose, you shouldn't try to play down his victory by calling him a 'rubber wall' or 'pusher'. It would be more sensible to look for a training partner against whom you can test your patience, concentration and intelligence.

6 He puts backspin and/or topspin on everything.

If he brings his arm up sharply on the forehand, and down sharply on the backhand, you must watch out.

The topspin forehand comes at you higher and faster than you expected after the bounce. You should therefore stand further back than usual to attack the ball and make contact with it when it is still in front of you.

After the topspin has reached its highest point, it drops very fast. You will have to watch this point, especially on his passing shots, which you believe to be going well out and which then land in the field of play.

The backspin backhand bounces more slowly and lower than a normal shot. You must therefore advance a little more than usual and bend your knees to return it.

Nine different players and how to play against them

Topspin and backspin shots lose their sting after they have reached the highest point of their bounce. They can therefore be easily returned when dropping. Deep, high topspin shots (which you must take when rising) are the exception, because they would otherwise force you back too far.

Try the occasional deep, high shot (which you can follow to the net), if he puts topspin on everything. You will notice that he will have a lot of trouble with it. Even balls he has to run for don't suit him.

7 He is the better player.

The decisive factor in a game against a superior opponent is your fighting spirit. If you start the game feeling all is lost and think you may manage to win, at the very most, two or three games, this (erroneous) conviction will probably prove right. Only if you enter the court with the firm intention of doing your very best, will you have a chance.

The first games are crucial. If you succeed in keeping the score even, his sense of security will be unexpectedly attacked. His shots will lose a lot of their original venom, because he will no longer hit them with quite so much confidence. An expected walk-over can turn into a real contest.

Do not attempt to reply to his hard shots with even harder returns, or to throw in drop shots as he does,

Nine different players and how to play against them

if you can't play them perfectly. *You mustn't try to play beyond the limits of your ability.*

If he plays *very fast,* simply position yourself about eighteen inches or one yard (forty-five centimetres to a metre) further back.

If he varies the pace, depth or spin of his shots, you must position yourself carefully to receive the ball. So keep your eye on it all the time.

3 He is left-handed.

There has always been a noticeably high quota of left-handed players among the top-class tennis stars. This is no coincidence: the left-handed player knows his opposite number's game exactly, whereas the right-handed player is faced with a closed book whenever he meets a left-handed opponent. It is accordingly of special value to occasionally train with someone who is left-handed.

The game of someone who is left-handed almost always has the same features:

an unpleasant service, since it is hit with a lot of slice or kick; a strong forehand, mostly with topspin; and a weaker backhand, mostly with backspin.

The difficulty lies in being able to take advantage of this last weakness. You will probably not

be able to do so with your backhand, as the backhand down the
line is a very difficult shot. It is
not worth trying it and making a
lot of unnecessary mistakes in the
attempt. Look only for good depth.

However, if you place your fore-
hands across the court *you* can
direct the course of the game.

If you want to attack, you should
make special use of your forehand, with which you can play
across court or down the line.

You must also think in 'reverse'
when serving. If you are serving
from the right-hand court by far
the best shot is a (slice) service
which bounces near the sideline
and opens up the whole court for
you. From the left-hand side, the
most advantageous shot is one
played down the centre service
line.

The following rule also holds good
when playing against left-handed
players: never play on blindly to
a specific plan or he will be able
to adapt his game to yours from
the very start.

*Pay real attention to the service
return.*

If he tosses the ball up to the right
(your left), be prepared for a kick
service, which will apparently
come at you, but will, in fact,
bounce high on to your forehand.

If he tosses the ball to the left (your right), he is serving with slice. The ball will bounce away from you on to your backhand. You must be specially prepared for this kind of service coming from the left hand side of the court.

His game has no special features.

You will not need to make any special plans to play against him.

Awkward Situations

Win the points that count.

In tennis the winner is not the one who scores the most, but the one who scores the decisive points.

Make an extra effort:

at 40 : 30 or your advantage, and you win the game;

at 15 : 30 or 30 : 40 or his advantage, and the struggle starts all over again;

immediately after a bitterly contested point: experience has shown that this situation is followed by a drop in concentration; and

during the first two games in the second set (for the same reason).

The extra effort will be rewarded.

The key moments vary from match to match.

Each match contested has its key moments, two or three points which, in retrospect, you know have been decisive.

Born winners have an instinct for such key moments. This is when they play their best tennis.

The following two examples illustrate that no universal rules can be laid down.

Awkward Situations

In the struggle against a superior opponent, the first games of a set are of particular importance.

They decide whether the match will turn into a serious contest or not.

You are leading by 5 games to 2, but you know full well that this score does not correspond to the real standard of play. In order to win the set you must now try twice as hard, since he has nothing more to lose and will play a much more relaxed game.

No unnecessary risks on set or match points.

Most players get tense when they reach set or match point in an important contest. You can minimise this tension by:

concentrating on the first service;

only using shots you can execute perfectly;

avoiding shots which require a lot of 'feel' for the ball (e.g., the drop shot or attacking lob); and by

using a long follow-through.

It is a good idea to play an attacking game on such points. You will shorten the rally and force your opponent (who is just as nervous as you are) to play a relatively risky shot.

Awkward Situations

Be determined to win the first match point while you are still two or three points ahead. An opportunity carelessly thrown away could cost you the match.

You are not on form: slow down the pace.

You are in despair because you can't find your usual form, so you try to force the tempo to get the match over quickly.

This is the usual reaction, and it is the wrong one. By forcing the pace you will make even more mistakes.

You must obviously slow down the pace to find your rhythm.

In such a situation the most important thing is to concentrate on successfully returning the ball and to remember the basic rules:

keep your eye on the ball;

stand correctly to receive the ball (with your weight on the balls of your feet, sway gently from side to side);

start your backswing early;

attack the ball;
remember the long follow-through.

Above all *fight!* If you try for every shot your performance, even on a bad day, could be moderately good

wkward Situations

how no signs of being
red.

If you are weary, mistakes creep
into your game: you position
yourself badly to receive the ball
and your concentration flags.

An effective method of minimising
these mistakes is to

slow down the pace so much with
high, deep shots, that after each
shot you can return to the centre of
the possible returns without too
much difficulty; and

to play only crosscourt because it
is the easier shot.

If your opponent is just as tired as
you are, you can try to wear him
down with a last offensive. Moving
forward is actually less tiring than
running from side to side. (Your
opponent could, of course, frustrate
this plan with high lobs.)

Under no circumstances should
you let him know (by gestures or
complaints) that your strength is
exhausted. The cunning
psychologist will act as if weariness
is no problem at all.

nfair decisions.

Bad decisions by the linesmen and
your opponent's lucky shots are
annoying. However, you will
probably both get an equal share
of luck over all.

Awkward Situations

The apparent unfairness will only have an effect if you allow yourself to be thrown off balance by taking your displeasure out on your opponent or the umpire.

One point will then turn into a whole series of disastrous points because you are letting that one incident prey on your mind.

Winning a match despite the unfavourable conditions is a double victory.

Wind, Sun, Bad Court Conditions

Adapt, don't give up.

Wind, dazzling sunshine and an uneven or slippery court are as much tennis-playing conditions as are a calm, overcast sky and a superb court.

Instead of letting yourself be influenced by comments like 'I can't play tennis under these conditions', or 'That's a potato field, not a tennis court', you should say to yourself: 'All the better for me, if you can't adjust to it! At any rate, I'm going to have a try!'

If you bear the following tips in mind, you will have every chance of turning even the most unfavourable conditions to your advantage. It would be ideal if, during training, you practised playing under all possible conditions.

Playing *with* the wind.

You will increase your chances of winning, if you play *with* the wind:

keep moving up and down on the balls of your feet;

go to meet the ball in plenty of time;

hit with lots of topspin;

aim at the half-court line; and

attack frequently.

Wind, Sun, Bad Court Conditions

Playing *into* the wind.

If you are playing *into* the wind, the basic rules are:

run back *in plenty of time*;

use a *short* backswing;

consciously hit *beyond the base-line*;

attack instead of defending at the back; and

(for advanced players) throw in some dropshots.

Playing into the sun.

When *serving into* the sun, there are three methods (used singly or combined) to avoid having to look directly at the sun:

toss the ball more to the left or to the right; and/or

alter the position of your feet; and/or

position yourself further to the left or to the right.

If you attack and your opponent constantly lobs into the sun, try short, attacking balls with plenty of spin aimed at his backhand. He will have great difficulty in playing over your head.

Deep shadows.

If isolated shadows impede your view, the only answer is to concentrate on the ball twice as hard.

Wind, Sun, Bad Court Conditions

Slippery court.

Uneven court.

If the court is slippery, you can throw your opponent off balance by varying the depth and spin of your shots and occasionally playing two consecutive shots into the same corner.

On wet courts, slice and drop shots are lethal, because they hardly bounce.

Take short steps and only advance to the net if you are sure of winning the point, because, when starting to run after playing a passing shot or a lob, you can easily slip.

If the court is uneven:

use short backswings; and advance to the net as often as possible: the uneven ground will disturb you less there.

Lost — What Now?

Analyse—don't moan.

You've lost the contest, a saddening event, but hardly world-shattering!

Now is not the time to lose face. It is the wrong moment for complaints and excuses, however justified they may seem. Your ecstatic opponent will only be able to muster a sympathetic smile, so you should not expect too much attention or commiseration.

Good common sense will free you from your dejection. By asking yourself why you lost you take a great step towards regaining your self-confidence. You are no longer preoccupied by the defeat, but by *why* you were defeated.

Having read this book, you are now in a position to make a successful assessment of your main faults.

For example:

'Too many of my first services landed in the net.'

'My forehand service return was too high or landed outside the field of play.'

'When playing to the baseline, I didn't get enough depth.'

'I made far more mistakes on my backhand than on my forehand.'

'The ball was frequently played over my head when I was at the net.'

Lost — What Now?

'I tried to place my passing shots too close to the sidelines, instead of playing straight at him and over him.'

Assessment by a third party.

If you experience difficulty in assessing your game yourself, you can ask a friend to do the job for you. He must watch your match carefully and write down his observations on the basis of the criteria in the following chart.

How your game is analysed.

First and foremost comes the analysis of your shots. (Your opponent's shots are only listed when they contribute to the evaluation of your game.)

If you are serving, your friend must enter all your first and second services in the corresponding box (Aces=A).

If, at the end of the contest, the section *First Service* looks like this,

	In the field of play (A=ace)	Out	Net
First Service	JHT JHAT JHT III	JHT IIII	JHT JHT JHT JHT JHT III

then out of a total of 60 attempts, you have only got 18 first services (30%) into the field of play, 33 (55%) landed in the net, and the remaining 9 (15%) went out.

Your opponent's services are not noted down to avoid complicating the analysis unnecessarily.

No other shots are noted unless they lead directly to a point for you or your opponent.

Lost — What Now?

The following example explains the individual boxes:

	Out	Own mishit	Net	Own Winning shot	Op'ent's mishits	Op'ent's Winning shot
Forehand Service Return	JHT JHT JHT I		IIII	JHT II	I	JHT III

Altogether, 36 forehand service returns led directly to points.

Of *your* returns:

16 went out (Out)

4 landed in the net (Net)

7 could not be reached (or only just touched) by your opponent (Own Winning Shot).

To summarize:

If your opponent is serving, your friend only needs to indicate (with a stroke) the shot leading to the point.

If you are serving, he must enter the first service, and, if this is a fault, the second as well, and the ball that gets the point.

Conclusions.

The chart will thus give you the following information:

1 For your service:

the percentage of first services
which land in the service box;
the proportion of services which
went out to the ones that went
into the net;
the double faults (divided into
out and net); and
the second services which were
too short (see opponent's
winning shots on the service
return).

2 For the rest of your strokes:
the number of your mishits;
the number of balls which went
out or went into the net;
the ratio of your mishits to your
winning shots;
the ratio of your mishits to your
opponent's mishits;
the ratio of your winning shots
to your opponent's winning
shots; and
the insufficient depth of your
forehand and backhand, the
exaggerated height of your shots,
the shortness of your lobs, the
exaggerated depths of your drop
shots (see opponent's winning
shots).

Conclusion.

The ball is now placed squarely in
your court; it is up to you whether
you want to make the same
mistakes again and again or, by
concentrating your training on the
faults discovered in your game,
work on your weaknesses with this
book. Opt for the latter! Success
and more enjoyment from the game
of tennis will be your reward.

Assessment by a Third Party

	In the service box (A=ace)	Out	Net

	Own mishit		Own winning shot	Opponent's mishit	Net
	Out	Net			Opponent's winning shot
First Service					
Second Service					
Forehand service return					
Backhand service return					
Forehand					
Backhand					
Forehand passing shot					
Backhand passing shot					
Lob					
Drop shot					
Half volley					
Forehand volley					
Backhand volley					
Smash					

Opponent

Date

Result

Glossary of Technical Terms

attacking shot

A shot behind which the player advances to the net.

centre of the possible returns

The point from which you have to run the same distance to reach either of your opponent's possible return shots.

chip

The racket is held out to the ball without any backswing (as on a volley). Often this is the only solution when faced with hard serves.

crosscourt

A ball hit over the net from one side of the court to the diagonally opposite side.

down the line

Parallel and close to the sideline.

follow-through

The swinging motion of the racket after the ball is struck.

kick service

The ball bounces high onto the backhand.

slice

A stroke with backspin, which bounces more slowly and lower than a normal shot.

topspin

A ball hit over the top to impart a forward rotation so that it comes at you fast and high.

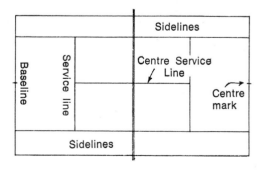

Bibliography

Books

Driver, H. I.	*Tennis Self-Instructor,* Madison, Wisconsin 1973
Gould, D.	*Tennis, anyone?* Palo Alto, California 1971
Harman, B.; Monroe, K.	*Use Your Head in Tennis,* Port Washington, New York 1966
Heldmann, G.; Lumiere, C.	*The Book of Tennis,* New York 1973
Jones, C. M.	*Tennis: How to Become a Champion,* London 1970
Jones, C. M.	*Improving Your Tennis, Strokes and Techniques,* London 1973
Kaufmann, A.	*Pardon, Me, Your Forehand is Showing,* New York 1956
Laver, R.; Collins, B.	*Rod Laver's Tennis Digest,* Northfield, Illinois 1973
Sonneman, D.	*The Compleat Pocket Tennis Strategist,* Boulder, Colorado 1973
Talbert, W. F. Old, B. S.	*The Game of Doubles in Tennis,* London 1957
Talbert, W. F. Old, B. S.	*The Game of Singles in Tennis,* Philadelphia and New York 1962
Talbert, W. F. Old, B. S.	*Stroke Production in the Game of Tennis,* Philadelphia and New York 1971

144